Made in the USA
Las Vegas, NV
09 June 2021

24439698R00029

Sailors use the bowline to fasten a sheet to a sail

Up through the rabbit hole,

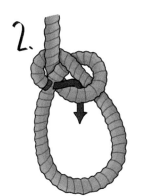

round the big tree;

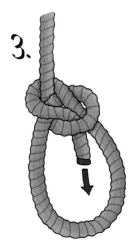

down through the rabbit hole and off goes he.

Wasserfrosh goes sailing

by Stas Holodnak

Illustrated by Jakub Grochola

The very first time Stas Holodnak saw the sea was as a little boy. He saw it from a bus window at the end of a bumpy twelve hour ride. The Black Sea appeared to him as blue as the sky itself only much crisper and within reach. Nowadays Stas lives in Brooklyn mere steps from the water. If he is not sailing - he is writing about it. Enter Wasserfrosh Goes Sailing - a book that explains sailing to children and parents. Have a question? Email Stas at stasholodnak@gmail.com.

Illustrations: Jakub Grochola

Book design: Ilya Startsev

Copyright © 2014 by Stas Holodnak

All rights reserved.

ISBN: 1502457253

ISBN-13: 978-1502457257

New York, USA

Upstream of Lake Paupack, in a small lily pond, there lived a young frog named Wasserfrosh.

One Friday afternoon Wasserfrosh biked to a frog village on the
northern edge of Lake Paupack to buy groceries. Every frog he met
on the way appeared upset. The store owner Kauffrosh himself
told Wasserfrosh the shocking news.

A Golden Lily, the frogs' most prized possession, was taken by a band of rowdy Toads. Song sparrows saw them rowing towards Toadsville, on the far side of Lake Paupack, in a great haste.

Wasserfrosh volunteered to recover the precious flower, but the village frogs were skeptical. No frog could out-row the toads, they said. What's more, a fearsome Northern Pike with a taste for frogs was known to roam in the mid-lake. Weary inhabitants of Lake Paupack were menaced by it or knew someone who was. Even noble swans would not leave their younglings alone for a moment. No Paupack frog dared to cross the pike and thus the lake - until now.

Wasserfrosh too was scared, but he knew where to get help. All of the Paupack toads working together could not match the power of the wind, and there was one frog who knew how to harness it.

That frog was his own uncle Fred Wasserfreud, who had just returned from an expedition to lake Wallenpaupack, which he circumnavigated in his sail boat called the Frigate.

After hearing what Wasserfrosh planned to do, his uncle agreed to help.

As the Frigate set sail across Paupack toward Toadsville, Fred shared sailing knowledge with his eager nephew. Here is what he told Wasserfrosh:

  "The very first thing to do when stepping on board of a sailboat is to put on a life jacket. You must wear it at all times! Just as you don't ride a bike without wearing a helmet, you don't go out on the water without wearing a life jacket. It's that simple."

"From now on," said Fred, "we shall refer to
   the front of a boat as the bow,
   the back of a boat as the stern,
   the left side of a boat as port,
   the right side as starboard.

The stick that you see in the stern is called a helm. You steer the Frigate with it.

When you move the helm to one side, the Frigate turns to the opposite side.

When you move the helm to starboard, the boat will turn to port.

When you move the helm to port, the boat will turn to starboard."

"Look," Fred pointed at a pole towering above the Frigate, "It's called a mast. The mast holds the sail upright.

The pole that supports the sail from below is called a boom. Together the mast, the boom and the sail make up a nice right triangle!

To raise the sail, we attach a rope to the upper corner of the sail. As we pull down on its free end, the rope pulls the sail up the mast. This rope is called the halyard. To hold the sail in place, we tie the free end of the halyard to the mast."

"What will happen if we untie the halyard?" asked Wasserfrosh.
"The sail will go down," said Fred,
"That's exactly what you do if you need to lower it."

Suddenly, the wind shook leaves in the trees around the lake - SHSHSH. The Frigate started to move fast - surprising Wasserfrosh a great deal.

"A sail is what keeps the Frigate moving," explained Fred.

"When the wind blows from behind, it simply pushes the sail forward - just like you would move forward if someone pushes you in the back.

It gets interesting when the wind is blowing sideways. The wind flows along both sides of the sail pushing and pulling it forward at the same time, making the boat move much faster!"

"Uncle Fred," asked Wasserfrosh, "you hold the helm to steer the Frigate, but why are you always holding a rope in your hand?"

"The rope I am holding is called the main sheet," Fred answered. "It's attached to the sail. By pulling the main sheet in or letting it out, you control how much wind is in the sail. This means you control how much power is in the sail and how fast it can pull the boat."

"The closer Frigate's bow is turned to the wind, the more sheet you pull in.

The farther the Frigate's bow is from the wind, the more sheet you let out. This is called trimming the sail. Many new sailors tend to pull the main sheet in too much. This slows down the boat.

Remember - when in doubt let it out!"

"But how do I know if I have trimmed the right amount?" asked Wasserfrosh.

"You'll feel it," Fred smiled. "When the boat starts to sail fast, you've trimmed the sail just right!"

Wasserfrosh was having a lot of fun. He trimmed the sail and he turned the helm over and over again. All of a sudden, the Frigate stopped moving.

"You cannot sail directly into the wind," Fred explained. "If you do, the boat will stall."

What if you need to get some place that is upwind?" asked Wasserfrosh.

"A straight line is not the only way to get from one place to another," said Fred.

"Say there is a tree between us and a pond. How do we get to the water?"

"We hop around the tree," said Wasserfrosh.

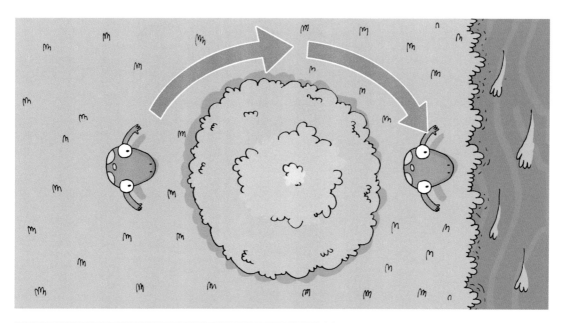

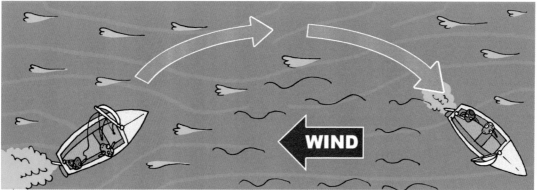

"Ai, so it is in sailing - the Frigate hops around the wind!"

"Wasserfrosh, take a close look at the Frigate," said Fred.
"Can you tell what side of the boat the wind is coming from?"

Wasserfrosh was sitting on the starboard side. He felt the breeze blowing at his back. "The wind is coming from the starboard side," he concluded.

"Yes," said Fred. "This means that the starboard side is now the windward side. The word windward means the first to the wind."

"What about the port side?" asked Wasserfrosh.

"The port side is now the leeward side," Fred answered. "The word 'lee' means away from the wind. The leeward side is easy to find - it's the one with the sail! The wind will always push the sail from the windward side of the boat over to the leeward side.

We, on our part, need to be on the windward side. This helps balance the boat."

"Look now," Fred continued, "as the Frigate turns through the wind, the starboard side will no longer be the windward side. The port side will be the first to the wind.

Can you tell what will happen to the sail?" asked Fred.

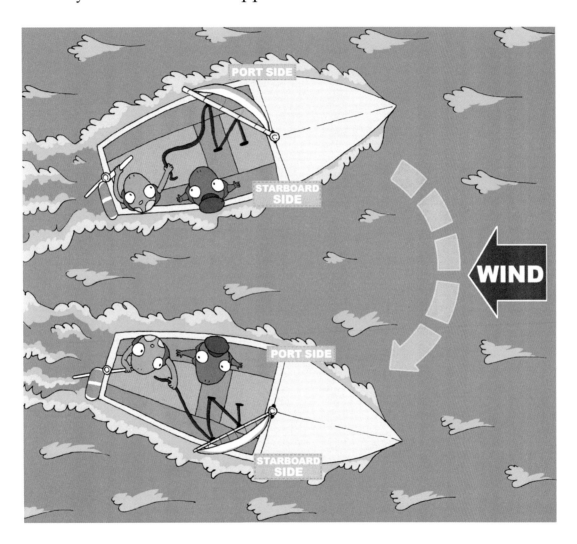

"The starboard side is the leeward side now. The wind will blow the sail over to it," said Wasserfrosh.

"Good answer, young sailor!" said Fred.

"You are ready to learn a new skill called tacking.

Tacking is something you do to turn the Frigate through the wind. Here is how you do it.

First - push the helm all the way to the leeward side, where the sail is. This will make the Frigate move in the opposite direction - toward the wind.

Second - pull the main sheet in all the way.

Third - as the wind swings the boom across the board, you duck and move to the new windward side.

Since the main sheet is pulled all the way in, it won't let the sail swing too far out.

Fourth - after the turn you straighten out the helm and let out the main sheet.

The more the Frigate turns away from the wind, the more sheet you let out.

Congratulations - you just completed your first tack! Here is an overview of the tack you just did.

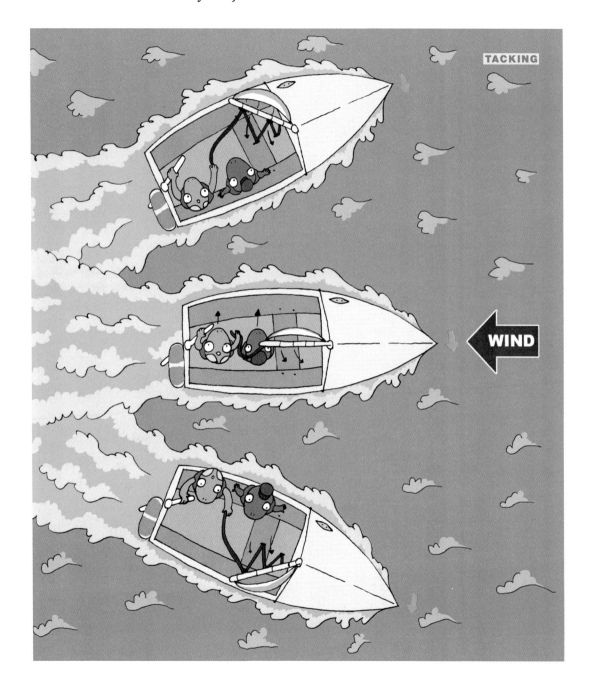

The other way for a boat to turn through the wind is called gybing. Gybing takes place when the Frigate crosses the wind with her stern and not with her bow.

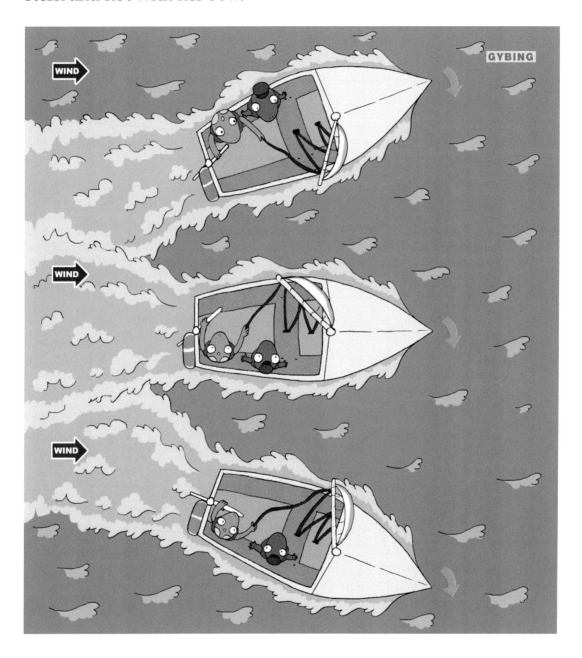

Wasserfrosh, you know how to handle the helm, the sail, and the main sheet," Fred concluded. "You will learn a lot more as you practice sailing. Remember, don't go out sailing alone. Always take a grown up sailor with you."

It was nighttime when Frigate reached Toadsville. The two frogs lowered the sail and patiently waited for a special time before sunrise when toads' dreams are the sweetest and their sleep is the deepest.

Early in the morning when warm vapor streams started to rise from the lake Paupack, Wasserfrosh entered Toadsville. Quick as lightning, he retrieved the Golden Lily and hopped back into the Frigate. The toads woke up then and chased the frogs. They rowed fast but they were no match for the Frigate. They fell out of sight in no time.

As soon as the Frigate entered the midlake, Wasserfrosh spotted something large lurking in the water. It was the fearsome Northern Pike himself! He quickly caught up with the Frigate. Anticipating a delicious meal, the pike's teeth snapped behind the Frigate's stern, missing it by only a hair.

A true sailor always thinks ahead. Fred steered the Frigate towards a narrow opening where water from Lake Paupack fed a creek down below.

The rocky and shallow bottom in that place forced water to move fast through it and then drop into the creek like a waterfall. When the Frigate's bow was no more than a few feet away from the creek, Fred pushed the helm toward the leeward side fast and hard. The Frigate turned windward and crossed the wind, leaving the waterfall behind.

As the wind pushed the sail and the boom across the board, Fred and Wasserfrosch ducked and moved to the windward side.

His eyes glued to the Frigate, the pike noticed the waterfall too late. The streaming, bubbling water seized the pike and pushed him down the creek - SPLASH!!!

"My hearties," said Fred to the song sparrows watching from above, "I declare Lake Paupack open to navigation." Just like that!

Every frog in the village was grateful to have the Golden Lily back.

Relieved Kauffrosh granted Wasserfrosh a ten percent discount on all of his future groceries. And Fred Wasserfreud started teaching sailing in the Paupack frog school. He still goes out exploring now and then.

Sailing Glossary

boom - a long, horizontal pole that supports a sail from below (page 12)

bow - the front side of a boat (page 8)

circumnavigate - sail all the way around (page 6)

downwind - the direction in which the wind is blowing

gybe - turn the stern of a boat into and through the wind (page 29)

halyard - a rope used for raising or lowering a sail (page 13)

helm - a piece of equipment you steer a boat with (page 9)

leeward side - the side of a boat that is second to the wind. The wind will push the sail over to the the leeward side. (page 23, 24)

life jacket - a vest that helps keep a person's head above water (page 7)

main sheet - a line that trims a sail (page 18)

mast - a tall, vertical pole that holds a sail (page 12)

port - the left side of a boat (page 8)

sail - a piece of material that catches the wind and moves a boat (page 12)

starboard - the right side of a boat (page 8)

stern - the back side of a boat (page 8)

tack - turn the bow of a boat into and through the wind (page 25, 26, 28)

trim the sail - pull in or let out the main sheet. Trimming controls how much wind a sail catches and how fast it can move a boat (page 18, 19)

upwind - against the direction of the wind, facing the wind (page 21)

windward side - the side of a boat that is facing the wind, first to the wind (page 22)

Knots

The Figure Eight Knot is used at the end of a line to keep it from slipping away.

A snake's tail makes a loopty loop

For the snake to slitter through

Wasserfrosh pulls on its head

The snake becomes a figure eight